Native
Trees

OF BRITISH COLUMBIA

Reese Halter and Nancy J. Turner

Illustrated by Stephen Pearce

Design by Wonder Inc.
Printed in Canada by C.J. Graphics Inc.

National Library of Canada Cataloguing in Publication

Halter, Reese.
   Native Trees of British Columbia / Reese Halter and
Nancy J. Turner; illustrated by Stephen Pearce.

   Includes bibliographical references.
   ISBN 0-9684143-3-8

   1. Trees–British Columbia–Identification.
   I. Turner, Nancy J., 1947-   II. Pearce, Stephen III. Title.
QK203.B7H23   2003
582.16'09711   C2003-902291-9
                                          CIP

**Funding for this entire project was provided by a grant from
Global Forest – Pure Science.® GF-18-1999-01**

We would like to thank Peter Corbett, Stephen Sillett and Robert VanPelt for
reviewing the manuscript and making helpful comments.

2 June 03

Native Trees of British Columbia

For Jocelyn,

Trees are

awesome!

Best wishes,

Dr. Reere

For my Dad, Aubrey J. Halter, who first introduced me to trees at a very young age; and has inspired my life-long dedication and thirst for knowledge of trees. *RH*

To the Aboriginal elders and plant specialists of the province who keep the knowledge of trees alive and pass it on to the children. *NJT*

TABLE OF CONTENTS

FORWARD

British Columbia represents one of the last of the world's forested frontiers. Many parts of the province – from the Great Bear Rainforest, to the Coast Mountains, to the boreal forest, are about as far removed from the general public's everyday life as one can imagine. Here you will find the largest and tallest trees in Canada. The native trees of British Columbia cover a wide range of climates and environments, from 2000 year-old cedars, festooned with the moss of a coastal rainforest, to the bigleaf maple growing in your back yard.

This concise guidebook to 49 of the most common native trees of the province will give everyone from experts to amateurs the information they need to identify the native trees they encounter. Maps, beautiful line drawings, and interesting facts about the trees and how the First Peoples made use of these trees all aid the reader to further discovery about the Native Trees of British Columbia.

January 2003

Dr. Robert VanPelt
College of Forest Resources
University of Washington
Seattle, WA

People have lived around trees and forests since their earliest beginnings. They have relied on trees, both directly and indirectly, for their survival. We still rely on trees as much as we ever did, but many of us who live in urban areas have lost touch with the trees of our home places. Even in rural communities, many children today cannot identify or name the common trees around them. When we lose familiarity with things, when we are unable to name them or to understand their role in the environment, we often forget how valuable they are to us, and we take them for granted. Just as the first step in getting to know somebody is to learn their name and how to recognize their face, so learning the names and features of trees will help people to get to know them better, and to better understand their value. That is the purpose of this book: to help British Columbians of all ages become more familiar with the indigenous or native trees of our province, and, ultimately to help us understand how dependent we are on these beautiful and functional lifeforms.

What is a forest?

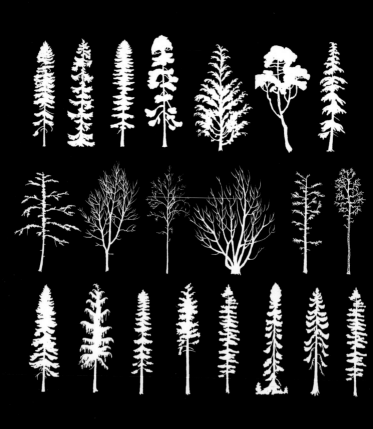

A forest is a complex ecosystem in which trees predominate. Trees grow all over the world, except where it is too cold, as on the tops of mountains or in the Arctic and Antarctic regions, where it is too dry, as in deserts, or where it is too wet, as in lakes, rivers and oceans. Forests are often described as *coniferous* (with cone-bearing, mainly evergreen needle-bearing trees like pines, spruces and firs), *deciduous* (with broad-leaved species that lose their leaves in the winter), or *mixed* (with both leafy and needle-bearing trees growing together). Forests are also named and classified by the major species of trees they include. We can talk about an "oak forest" or a "Douglas-fir forest," if these are the most common trees. Major vegetation zones are also named after the major tree species they support. In British Columbia, 14 major vegetation zones, called "biogeoclimatic zones," are recognized. All but two of these are named after major tree species that grow within them. For example, on southeastern Vancouver Island and the Gulf Islands, there is the Coastal Douglas-fir Biogeoclimatic Zone, and in the dry interior, there is the Ponderosa Pine Biogeoclimatic Zone.

A forest is not just made up of trees. It includes all the other plants that grow in it — shrubs, herbaceous (non-woody) plants, and mosses — as well as mushrooms, other fungi, bacteria and lichens. Forest ecosystems also include insects, birds, and other animals. The trees of the forest provide important habitat for all the other species. They help to absorb heavy rainfall and snowfall, they provide shade and moderate the temperature, and they offer physical shelter, water and nutrients to help the other species survive.

Fire, insect infestations and strong winds that uproot trees are all natural disturbances that occur within Canadian forests. They are important because they assist in decomposing old forests and they help make new forest soils. Disturbances also create new regenerated forests. Forests provide resources for a variety of species at different times throughout the perpetual cycle of life.

Humans use the forest in many different ways. Trees and other forest plants provide us with oxygen to breathe and with clean water. They also help to filter out pollution. Of course, the forest provides us with wood for many different purposes: fuel, construction, and pulp and paper. Forests also contain many edible species, including the inner bark of certain trees, as well as fruits, edible green shoots, and edible mushrooms. We get many materials from the forest besides wood: pitch for glue, turpentine for paint thinner, bark and leaves for dye, and bark for basket-making. People also rely on the forests for numerous kinds of medicine. The sounds and scents of forests, and their colours and textures, all give us pleasure and delight. Artists and musicians and many other people find inspiration from forests.

Unfortunately, we are cutting down our forests too quickly, so we can sell the timber, or clear the land for agriculture, roads, and buildings. The world's wild forests have decreased drastically in the last hundred years or so. Removing forests, for whatever purpose, is called *deforestation*. If deforestation continues at its present rate, we will be much poorer in the long run. It is very hard to replace a forest. We can plant more trees, but forests are so complex, we cannot easily restore all the different animal and plant species once they have disappeared.

Classifying Forests

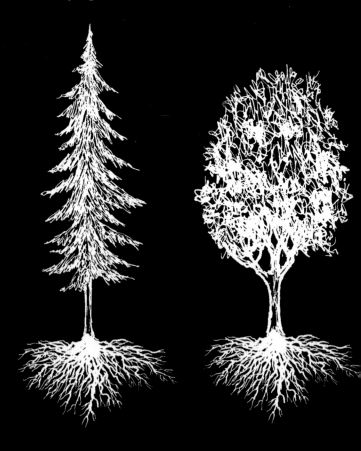

Trees are the tallest, biggest and oldest plants in the world that are able to support themselves. In height, they are matched or surpassed only by the vines that climb them, or by some types of marine algae called kelps that grow very long but are supported by the water. Trees typically grow from a single erect main woody trunk with branches growing from it. The trunk and branches are covered with bark that protects the growing tissues underneath. Every year, the trunk grows bigger and the tree gets taller until it is fully mature. The tallest trees exceed 110 m in height – as tall as a 36-storey-building.

People generally divide trees into coniferous and broadleaf species. Conifers bear their seeds in cones, usually protected by woody scales. They have leaves that are long and thin, that are called "needles," or small and scale-like. Most of the broadleaf trees are flowering plants or angiosperms, and they bear flowers and have their seeds protected in enclosed fruits of one kind or another. Their leaves are usually wide and flat. In Northern Hemisphere temperate regions, broadleaf trees are almost all deciduous, meaning that they drop their leaves in the wintertime, while most conifers are evergreen, meaning they keep their leaves over several years and always stay green. However, there are always exceptions. In British Columbia, the larches *(Larix)* are conifers that shed their needles each winter, and Arbutus

(Arbutus menziesii) is a broadleaf evergreen. It keeps its leaves over the winter, but it sheds its bark in paper-thin sheets every year. Pacific yew *(Taxus brevifolia)* is a conifer whose seeds are not produced in cones, but are surrounded by a fleshy berry-like cup, called an aril.

Some large plants that are not actually woody, like palms and banana plants, are also considered to be trees. So are some large kinds of ferns, called "tree-ferns." Millions of years ago, there were other kinds of plants that grew tall and tree-like; these were the ancient relatives of horsetails and clubmosses.

A habitat with many trees growing together is a forest. Forests are home for many different species of plants and animals. Humans depend on trees and forests in many different ways. In British Columbia, The First Peoples rely on forests for a variety of foods, materials and medicines. The forests are also important spiritually, and trees and other plants, as well as the animals of the forest, are recognized for their ability to influence human lives. They help and support those who respect them and care for them, but they can harm those who are disrespectful and wasteful. There are many stories about trees helping humans to survive. For example, in the traditions of the Saanich First Peoples of southern Vancouver Island, there was a great flood long ago. The waters rose and rose to the highest points of land. Some people went into their canoes and anchored themselves to an Arbutus tree at the top of a mountain called LAUWELNAW (Mount Newton). The Arbutus held them onto the rocky hilltop until the waters receded. Because the Arbutus saved them so long ago, the Saanich have always held this tree in great reverence and they do not usually burn it as a fuel.

People have relied on many different types of wood for fuel, both for cooking and for keeping themselves warm. Western redcedar *(Thuja plicata)* makes good kindling, for starting a fire, and the shredded inner bark of this tree was used as a tinder, to help ignite the fire. Douglas-fir *(Pseudotsuga menziesii)* wood and bark are excellent, hot-burning fuels. Western hemlock *(Tsuga heterophylla)* burns slowly, and is good to keep a fire going overnight. The wood of red alder *(Alnus rubra)* is considered to be the very best fuel for smoking fish and meat; many still use it in their smokehouses today.

In addition to using wood for fuel, the First Peoples of British Columbia are renowned for their woodworking and carving skills. The items they produce from the trees of the forest are prime examples of the integration of art and utility. Peoples' survival completely depended upon trees. From the largest of dugout canoes, skillfully crafted from giant logs of western redcedar and capable of carrying 60 people, to the smallest fish-hook made from the tough knots of western hemlock, wood was a mainstay of peoples' cultures and lifeways. The forests of the province offer a wide range of tree species, each with its own specific characteristics and potential applications. Western redcedar is perhaps the best known and most versatile, being used not only for canoes of many sizes and styles, but also for totem poles, house posts and planks, and numerous smaller items. It is soft, rot-resistant, and easily worked. Woodworkers used sharp-bladed adzes and chisels to fashion and smooth the wood; nowadays, many use power tools as well. People used to be able to split long planks of cedar for their houses from standing, live trees, using stone mallets and wooden wedges. Among the most remarkable examples of wood-

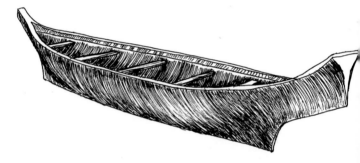

A western redcedar dugout canoe.

working are the amazing bentwood storage boxes of the Northwest Coast. The four sides of these amazing containers are made from a single western red-cedar board, grooved or kerfed across its grain at three, carefully measured points, then soaked or steamed until soft, and bent along the groove at right-angles to form the three corners of the box. The fourth corner, where the ends of the board come together, is pegged or stitched with tough root strands of spruce *(Picea)* or western redcedar. The box is tightly fitted with a base and a lid and is often carved in relief or painted with distinctive geometric representations of animals or supernatural beings. Bentwood boxes, used for cooking, transport and storage, were formerly a part of every household's possessions. They were widely exchanged as gifts or trade goods, filled with food like Pacific crabapples *(Malus fusca)* and highbush cranberries *(Viburnum edule)* stored in water or oil.

Other types of wood had their own particular applications. Pacific yew wood is known for its toughness and resiliency. It was used to make implements that were subjected to tremendous pressure, like bows, wedges, harpoon shafts, clubs and root-digging sticks. Pacific crabapple wood was also known for its springiness and toughness, whereas red alder was known for its smooth, even grain and was used for carving dishes, dance masks and spoons. Black cottonwood *(Populus balsamifera* ssp. *trichocarpa)* logs were sometimes fashioned into dugout canoes to be used for transportation in the interior lakes and rivers. Yellow cedar *(Chamaecyparis nootkatensis)* is strong smelling, so couldn't be used around food, but was known as an excellent wood for making canoe paddles, as was bigleaf maple *(Acer macrophyllum)* wood. The latter was named "paddle-tree" in some of the coastal languages. Bigleaf maple wood was also used for the carved, plate-sized disks of spindlewhorls, which Salish weavers used to spin mountain goat or dog wool for blankets. The hard, flexible wood of vine maple *(Acer circinatum)* and Rocky Mountain maple *(A. glabrum)* was used for snowshoe frames and drum hoops. Douglas-fir sapling wood was used for spear shafts and dipnet poles. In short, every wood had its value.

Today, although First Peoples do not rely on wood to the same extent as their ancestors did, woodcrafting arts are still integral to peoples' lives, and woodcarvers are held in high esteem. Masks, bowls and traditional representations of animals are still used in First Peoples ceremonies, and are high value items available for sale at many art galleries and giftshops throughout the Northwest Coast region.

First Peoples made many other important items from tree products. As well as its wood, the fibrous bark, roots and branches of western redcedar were valued for making baskets. The bark of western redcedar and yellow cedar was also woven into mats, blankets, hats and clothing. Sheets of white birch bark *(Betula papyrifera)* were, and still are, made into baby cradles, packbaskets and other containers, as well as into bark canoes. Bark sheets of Engelmann spruce *(Picea engelmannii)*, subalpine fir *(Abies lasiocarpa)*, and western white pine *(Pinus monticola)* were also used for baskets and canoes in some areas. Roots of Sitka spruce *(Picea sitchensis)* and white spruce *(P. glauca)* were used in basketry. The Haida and Tlingit of the North Coast make exquisitely fine twined baskets and hats of Sitka spruce-root. People also sometimes made baskets, trays and bags from the inner bark of Rocky Mountain maple. They used the tough, stringy bark of bitter cherry *(Prunus emarginata)* and pin cherry *(P. pensylvanica)* for wrapping the joints of implements to strengthen and waterproof them, and to decorate baskets. They used the bark of red alder and its relatives to make a red dye for colouring cedar-bark and other materials. Trees also provided food for people. On the coast, the small, tart apples from Pacific crabapple were a favourite fruit. In the mountains of the southern Interior, the Plateau Peoples sought the large, wingless seeds of whitebark pine *(Pinus albicaulis)*, a timberline species, roasted them and ate them as a favourite snack. People also harvested the edible cambium tissue of certain kinds of trees.

This is the soft growing layer between the wood and bark, which is thick and juicy in the late spring, when the sap is running. On the coast, they ate the cambium of western hemlock, Sitka spruce, red alder and black cottonwood. In the interior, it was mainly lodgepole pine *(Pinus contorta var. latifolia)* and ponderosa pine *(P. ponderosa)* cambium. The harvesters would remove a rectangular section of bark from the trunk, scrape the edible tissue off the wood or the inside of the bark, and then eat it fresh or in some cases, dry it for winter use.

Another very important aspect of forests and trees is their gift of medicines. The sticky pitch, or resin of some trees, especially the coniferous trees, is known to have antibiotic properties, and was used to make a salve for burns, cuts, wounds, or slivers. People also made many other medicines from different kinds of tree barks, as well as from the leaves, flowers, and other parts of trees. One of the best known tree-derived medicines is taxol, extracted from the bark of Pacific yew and now widely used to treat ovarian and other types of cancer, heart disease and AIDS. First Peoples have been using Pacific yew bark as a medicine for thousands of years.

People wishing to use medicines from the forest, however, need to be very cautious, because Pacific yew and some other trees are toxic. The medicines must be prepared and prescribed by people who have special knowledge and understanding of the dosages and circumstances for their use.

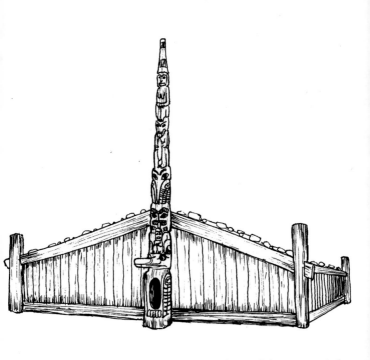

A First Peoples longhouse made from western redcedar.

Guide to Identification

HERE ARE SOME TERMS THAT ARE USED TO DESCRIBE TREES AND OTHER PLANTS OF THE FOREST:

APPEARANCE

Attention! Size and shape can vary tremendously, particularly with type of environment and forest density. *Small* in this book means less than 20 m; *Medium* means about 20-40 m; *Tall* means about 40-60 m; *Very Tall* means more than 60 m.

OCCURRENCE

This means where a tree can be found, or where we might expect it to grow. Some trees, like Garry oak *(Quercus garryana)*, prefer relatively dry, open areas, and others, like western redcedar, usually grow in moist soil and can tolerate shade. The range of a tree species is also important; this is the extent of its distribution. For example, Douglas-fir grows along the coast of British Columbia from Vancouver Island and the Lower Mainland, to the central coast, around the Kitlope Valley, but it does not occur on Haida Gwaii or around Prince Rupert. Its range extends eastward to the Rocky Mountains, and northward in the interior to the Cariboo and Chilcotin regions and southward to Creston and Grand Forks.

Twigs, conifer (left) and broadleaf (right).

Lenticels on cherry bark.

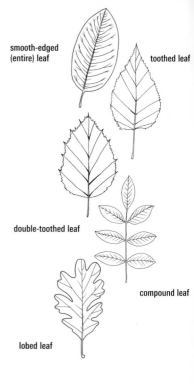

smooth-edged (entire) leaf

toothed leaf

double-toothed leaf

compound leaf

lobed leaf

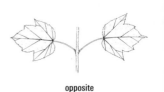

alternate

opposite

TWIGS

Small branches or shoots growing from the trunk or branches of a tree or shrub.

BARK

– is the rough, hard outer covering of the branches and trunks of trees and other woody plants. It protects the living tissues of the tree from damage and water loss. The bark is often divided into an outer layer of hard, dead cells, and inner bark with cells that are still living and functioning and carry sugars to the roots from the leaves.

LEAVES (SINGULAR LEAF)

Flat green structures of various shapes that grow from the stems or branches of trees and other plants, and whose main function is photosynthesis, the conversion of the sun's energy to chemical energy stored in carbohydrates and other organic molecules. The shape, size, texture and other physical features of leaves, and their arrangement (opposite, alternate and whorled) on the stems or branches are all characteristics that help in identifying trees and other plants

LENTICELS

– are special elongated areas on the bark of some trees (e.g. cherry, birch) which function in gas exchange.

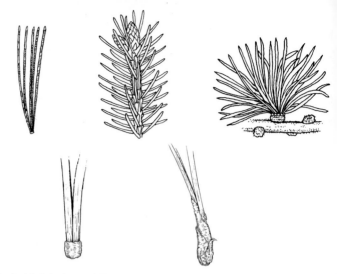

Needles (clockwise from top left), pine, spruce, larch, pine fasicle 2nd year, pine fasicle 1st year.

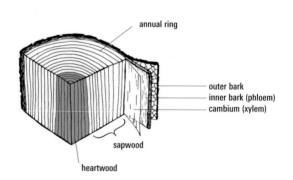

annual ring

outer bark
inner bark (phloem)
cambium (xylem)

sapwood

heartwood

NEEDLES

– are long, slender, usually tough and aromatic leaves of coniferous trees. They usually stay on the trees for several years (except for larch and a few other species). Sometimes they are borne singly, sometimes in clusters of two to many together, as in pines, larches and true cedars *(Cedrus)*.

CAMBIUM

– is a layer of living cells surrounding plant cells that in trees is located between the wood and bark. It produces the new growing tissues, particularly the sap-conducting tissues called xylem (water and nutrients) and phloem (food – made by the leaves), and ultimately, in trees, the wood and the bark. The nutrient-rich cambium of some trees was used as food by First Peoples, and is also eaten by bears and other animals.

FRUITS

– are the seed-containing structures of flowering plants. Technically, these are ripened ovaries and associated tissues. Fruits may be fleshy, like apples or peaches, or dry, as in maple fruits (called samaras). They may contain a single seed e.g. cherry or many seeds e.g. apple. Nuts and acorns are also fruits, and so are grains of grasses. Some coniferous trees, like Pacific yew and juniper *(Juniperus)*, bear their seeds in fruit-like structures, but these

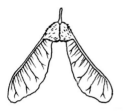 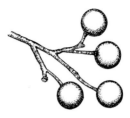

Fruits (left to right), maple samara and bitter cherries.

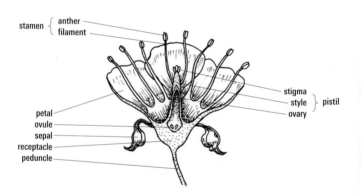

stamen $\left\{ \begin{array}{l} \text{anther} \\ \text{filament} \end{array} \right.$

$\left. \begin{array}{l} \text{stigma} \\ \text{style} \\ \text{ovary} \end{array} \right\}$ pistil

petal
ovule
sepal
receptacle
peduncle

The typical parts of a flower.

are botanically different from true fruits because the seeds are not fully enclosed at maturity.

FLOWERS

– are the reproductive organs of flowering plants, including the broadleaved trees in this book. Some plants contain both female reproductive parts (ovaries, containing ovules or immature seeds) and male reproductive parts (anthers, bearing pollen) in one flower; these are called *perfect* flowers. Others have separate female and male parts, borne in different flowers, or sometimes even on different plants. If the seed flowers and pollen flowers occur on different trees then they are called "dioecious"; if they occur on the same tree then they are called "monoecious." For seeds to be produced, pollen from the male part of the flower must reach and "pollinate" the female part of the flower. The pollen grows a tube down to the ovule in the female flower, and fertilizes the ovule, which will then mature and grow into a seed. In some plants, like willow *(Salix)* and alder *(Alnus)*, the pollen is carried to the female flower on the wind. The flowers of these plants are usually greenish and not very conspicuous. Other plants attract insects – bees, butterflies or beetles – or even hummingbirds, to help carry their pollen. Flowers of these plants are usually showy, with coloured petals and sweet nectar to entice the pollinators. Arbutus flowers are pollinated by insects.

Parts of a conifer cone:

cone scale

bract

seed with wing

Douglas-fir cone

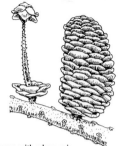

Abies cone with a bare axis
remaining after seed dispersal.

Male and female cones.
Young female hemlock cone (above).
Male pollen cones (below).

32

SEED CONE

Coniferous trees produce their seeds in cones. These vary in size from a tiny western redcedar cone, about 1 cm long, to a western white pine cone, which can be 25 cm long. The seed cone consists of a central axis or rachis, surrounded by usually flattened woody scales, sometimes interlayered with bracts. In Douglas-fir cones, the bracts are prominent and three-pointed. They look like the back feet and tails of tiny mice who are squeezing themselves headfirst between the scales. The seeds are produced on the scales, and when the cones are mature, and the weather conditions are right the scales (in most cases) will open up and release the seeds. Most coniferous tree seeds have a little papery wing attached to them to help them catch the wind when they are whirling down to the ground; this helps to disperse them further from the parent tree. The seed cone is the female cone. Coniferous trees also have male cones that are usually quite small, inconspicuous, and not woody like the female cones. The male cones produce the pollen and then usually drop off the tree.

British Columbia

Atlin

Fort Nelson

Stewart

Hudsons Hope • • Ft. St. John
• Dawson Creek

Haida Gwaii

Mackenzie

Prince Rupert
Smithers
Masset
Terrace
Burns Lake • Ft. St. James
Kikimat
Queen Charlotte
Vanderhoof • • Prince George

Quesnel

Bella Coola

Williams Lake

Golden

Port Hardy
Cache Creek • Revelstoke
Lilloet
Salmon Arm
Kamloops
Campbell River
Vernon
Powell River
Merritt
Kelowna
Kimberley
Penticton
Fern
Port Alberni
Vancouver
Castlegar
Cranbro
Nanaimo
Hope
Princeton
Nelson
Trail
Creston

N

Victoria

36

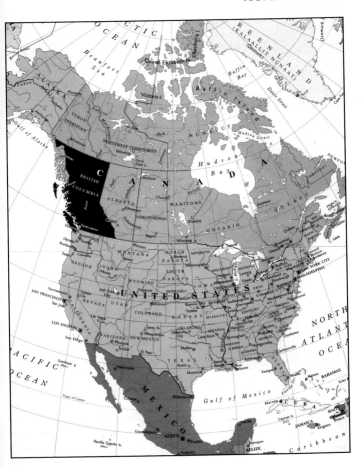

THE CONIFERS

(Pinus monticola Dougl.
ex D. Don)

western white pine

APPEARANCE: Very tall trees up to 65 m high, can live for 600 years; recognizable from afar as branches "stick-out" of the upper crown.

OCCURRENCE: Vancouver Island - from Port Hardy southward and adjacent on Mainland mountains. Common in SE BC's cedar-hemlock forests including Kootenay and Arrow Lakes, Shuswap and as far north as Quesnel Lake. On the coast, trees grow near to the subalpine, in the interior only to about 1000 m.

BARK: Thin, grayish green when young; with age darkens, develops distinct patterns of small thick plates.

LEAVES: Needles 5 - 12.5 cm, soft, edges finely toothed, bundles of 5; longer than either limber or whitebark pine.

SEED CONE: Slightly curved and cylindrical; 2 years to ripen; the longest of any BC pines.

WOOD: Moderately strong, creamy white to yellow in colour; good for carving, commercial timber.

FIRST PEOPLES: Sheets of the bark were used to make canoes by the Ktunaxa and other First Peoples. The fragrant pitch is used to make a medicinal salve for sores and cuts.

TREE FACTS: Suffers an introduced European fungus, disease called white pine blister rust; "*monticola*" means inhabiting the mountains; soft needles make a comfortable mattress when sleeping in the woods.

whitebark pine

(Pinus albicaulis Engelm.)

APPEARANCE: Small tree up to 20 m high, more usually recognizable as stunted multistemmed tree; can live over 1000 years.

OCCURRENCE: Occurs widely in the southern half of BC in Coast Mountains, and eastward into Rockies at elevations of 1000 m and above. This frost tolerant subalpine tree grows to the treeline on rocky soils, rock ledges and cliff faces.

BARK: Whitish, thin, and smooth on young trees; brown to reddish with loosely, scaly plates on older trees.

LEAVES: Needles 4-8 cm, stiff with slight curve, edges smooth, bundles of 5; clustered towards the end of the twig.

SEED CONE: Egg-shaped, sticky with resin; 2 years to ripen, cones ripped apart by Clark's Nutcrackers and ground squirrels; wingless seeds.

WOOD: Moderately soft, pale brown to white in colour.

FIRST PEOPLES: The large, nut-like seeds were a favourite food; sometimes children climbed the trees to harvest the cones, which were roasted in a fire or an oven until they could be broken open to obtain the seeds. These were cracked and eaten like peanuts.

TREE FACTS: Suffers from blister rust disease; co-evolved with bird - Clark's Nutcracker, relies upon birds to disperse its seeds; important source of food for ground squirrels, black and grizzly bears; *albicaulis* means "white stem."

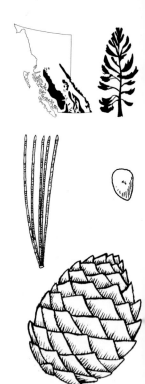

(Pinus flexilis James)*

limber pine

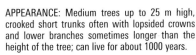

APPEARANCE: Medium trees up to 25 m high, crooked short trunks often with lopsided crowns and lower branches sometimes longer than the height of the tree; can live for about 1000 years.

OCCURRENCE: Limited only to the high slopes of the southern Rocky Mountains at 1000 m and above. This frost tolerant subalpine tree grows to the treeline on rocky soils, rock ledges and cliff faces.

BARK: Pale gray and smooth on young trees; dark brown, thick rough bark with scaly plates as trees age.

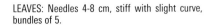

LEAVES: Needles 4-8 cm, stiff with slight curve, bundles of 5.

SEED CONE: Cylindrical and two to three times larger than those of whitebark pine; 2 years to ripen; Clark's Nutcrackers (birds) disperse wingless seeds.

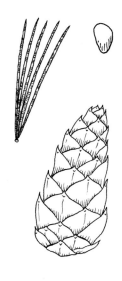

WOOD: Moderately soft, yellow to nearly white in colour.

FIRST PEOPLES: High protein seeds were used as food source, where available.

TREE FACTS: Suffers from blister rust disease, named after its "flexible" branches, this species is the rarest of all the native BC pines.

ponderosa pine

(Pinus ponderosa Dougl. ex P. & C. Laws.)

APPEARANCE: Tall tree up to 49 m high; flat-topped with age; can live up to 650 years.

OCCURRENCE: Found in valley bottoms and slopes up to about 1000 m in Okanagan and Similkameen Valleys; extends into the Caribou just north of Clinton; in lower Arrow and Kootenay Lakes, Kootenay River Valley north to Columbia Lake; SW BC as far as Skagit Valley.

BARK: Dark, plate-like scales on young trees; older trees are reddish with deep furrows (thick bark protects tree from surface fires), butterscotch-like aroma, scales look like pieces of jigsaw puzzle.

LEAVES: Needles are 12-25 cm, straight, stiff but flexible, bundles in 3; longest of all BC pines.

SEED CONE: Reddish brown, oblong, prickly, 2 years to ripen; falls to the ground in the winter.

WOOD: Moderately strong and hard, yellowish to nearly white in colour; commercial timber.

FIRST PEOPLES: In the springtime the inner bark of young trees was scraped off the wood and eaten; some people also ate the seeds, which are also enjoyed by squirrels; the needles were used to line underground food storage pits; pitch was used to make a medicinal salve.

TREE FACTS: Cones and bark scales make hot quick fires; named "ponderosa" by explorer-botanist David Douglas because of its great size; drought resistant tree.

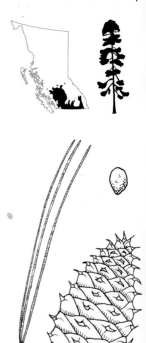

42

(*Pinus contorta* Dougl. ex Loud. var. *latifolia* Engelm.)

lodgepole pine

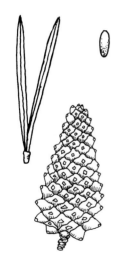

APPEARANCE: Medium tree up to 40 m high, straight trunk with narrow conical crown; can live for about 250 years.

OCCURRENCE: Widespread throughout BC; common in mid-mountain, less common in subalpine.

BARK: Dark gray to orange-brown, thin with small loose scales.

LEAVES: Needles are 3-7 cm, bundles of 2, usually twisted, stiff, sharply pointed, sharp toothed edges.

SEED CONE: Oval cone, 3-6 cm long, curved, prickly, remains closed on tree for up to 20 years.

WOOD: Moderately hard and heavy; pale in colour; straight grained; important commercial timber.

FIRST PEOPLES: Inner bark important as food source, harvested in long strips in the late spring; sometimes called "pine noodles"; pitch (pine sap) used as ingredient in many medicines; poles important for construction of dwellings, or lodges.

TREE FACTS: Most widespread conifer in BC, well adapted to forests fires – abundant seed cones open after the heat of the fire and provide seed for new forest.

shore pine

(Pinus contorta Dougl. ex.
Loud. var. *contorta)*

APPEARANCE: A medium tree 25 m high; twisted and crooked form, often with bushy and irregular branches.

OCCURRENCE: Throughout coastal BC from sea level to about 650 m; thrives on rocky ridges, coastal sand dunes and in bogs.

BARK: Reddish brown plates, thicker than lodepole pine; develops deep furrows with age.

LEAVES: Needles are 3-5 cm, bundles of 2, usually twisted, stiff, sharply pointed, dark green.

SEED CONE: Oval and 3-5 cm long, curved, prickly, 2 years to ripen; open when mature but can remain on the tree.

WOOD: Light wood; moderately strong; sometimes with twisted grains, non commercial.

FIRST PEOPLES: Pitch (pine sap) and bark used as medicines; the wood is used as a fuel.

TREE FACTS: Named after crooked twisted shape of the trees; tolerant of salt spray (from the ocean) and very poor soil conditions; not as well adapted to fire as lodgepole pine; bark can be peeled off and used to make an emergency cast for a broken arm or leg.

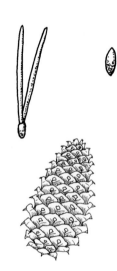

(Pinus banksiana Lamb.) # Jack pine

APPEARANCE: A small tree up to 18 m high; slender, straight with little taper; small crown; trees can live for about 200 years.

OCCURRENCE: Northeastern corner of BC from Mackenzie Valley just south of Northwest Territories in Canada's most northern and extensive forest type called the "boreal forest."

BARK: Reddish brown to gray when young; furrowed and platey, becoming dark brown with age.

LEAVES: Needles are 1-4 cm long, bundles of 2; straight or slightly twisted and edges toothed.

SEED CONE: Oval, 3-7 cm long; curved but sometimes straight, non prickly; 2 years to ripen; remains closed on tree for up to 18 years.

WOOD: Moderately hard and heavy; light brown; used for construction and pulp.

FIRST PEOPLES: Inner bark used as an important food source especially in early springtime; pitch (pine sap) used as medicine.

TREE FACTS: Well adapted to forests fires – abundant seed cones open after the heat of the fire and provide seed for new forest; fossil evidence shows that 9,000 years ago this tree was found as far south as North Carolina, USA.

western larch

(Larix occidentalis Nutt.)

APPEARANCE: A very tall tree up to 65 m, straight with slight taper, short branches and crowns; trees can live for about 500 years.

OCCURRENCE: Low to mid mountains; mixed drier cedar-hemlock forests of Columbia Mountains south of Shuswap Lake and in the Douglas-fir-lodgepole pine forests east of Lake Okanagan.

BARK: Scaly and reddish-brown when young; orange red, thick with furrows and flaky as ages; thick bark protects older trees from surface fires.

LEAVES: 15-30 needles (3-5 cm long) per cluster; clusters raised from twigs on "spur shoots"; deciduous, spectacular shades of yellow in the autumn before all needles are shed.

SEED CONE: Oval to egg shaped, 3-5 cm long, tail-like "bracts" longer than cone scales.

WOOD: Strong and hard, brown to yellowish in colour; excellent construction timber.

FIRST PEOPLES: Bark and leaves used in medicines; sweet tasting gummy sap used for chewing; when the needles turn yellow in the fall, it is a sign that the bears are ready to go into their dens.

TREE FACTS: Older trees with thick bark are well adapted to fire; tallest species of larch in the world; grouse often eat the fallen needles.

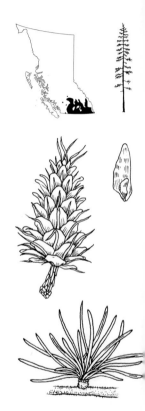

(Larix lyallii Parl.)

subalpine larch

APPEARANCE: Medium trees up to 28 m high; mostly gnarled, short, sturdy, tapering rapidly, ragged crown, irregular spaced branches; can live for over 900 years.

OCCURRENCE: Makes up thin band of upright trees growing to the treeline in mountains of the Cascades also including Manning, Cathedral Lake parks; Selkirks, Monashees, Purcells, and Rockies.

BARK: Thin, smooth, yellowish when young; becoming thicker, reddish-brown and scaly with age.

LEAVES: 30-40 needles (3-5 cm long) per cluster; clusters raised from twigs on "spur shoots"; deciduous, awesome shades of yellow in the autumn before all needles are shed.

SEED CONE: Elliptic shaped, 4-5 cm long; hairy, tail-like "bracts" longer than cone scales.

WOOD: Heavy and hard; non commercial tree.

FIRST PEOPLES: Boiled young twigs used for tea; a source of vitamin C.

TREE FACTS: In an emergency, back-country walkers can make soup from the young twigs; extremely frost tolerant tree.

tamarack

(Larix laricina (Du Roi) K. Koch)

APPEARANCE: Small trees up to 18 m high; slender trunk, straight, narrow crown, long branches; can live for over 200 years.

OCCURRENCE: In bogs, swamps and lower mountain slopes, primarily northeastern BC, found in patches in central interior of the province in the Nechako Valley, south of Vanderhoof and isolated trees west of Quesnel.

BARK: Smooth, gray and thin when young; reddish-brown and scaly with age.

LEAVES: 13-60 needles (2-5 cm long) per cluster; clusters raised from twigs on "spur shoots"; deciduous, tremendous shades of "smokey gold" in the autumn before all needles are shed.

SEED CONE: Oval shaped, 1-2 cm long; tail-like "bracts" shorter than cone scales; easily distinguished from either subalpine or western larches.

WOOD: Heavy and hard; minor commercial tree.

FIRST PEOPLES: The pitch or larch sap combined with grease served as cosmetics for skin or hair.

TREE FACTS: *Larix* comes from Latin "lar" meaning fat because the tree produces a lot of resin; tamarack occurs in every province and territory of Canada; can withstand temperatures of –55°C.

(Picea glauca (Moench) Voss)

white spruce

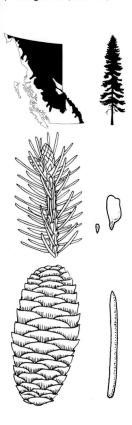

APPEARANCE: From gnarled, stunted trees up to 40 m high; from ragged, irregular to exquisite spiral-like crowns of stands in northern BC; branches bushy, horizontal but occasionally sloping downward in lower crown; can live for over 300 years.

OCCURRENCE: Low to mid-elevation forests of northern BC extends as far south as Lillooet, Cache Creek and Vernon; not found in Coast Mountains; Big Bend area of the Columbia River and scattered southwards along Rocky Mountains into Sparwood and Crowsnest Pass region.

BARK: Thin, light gray, smooth when young; darker gray with age, becoming scaly.

LEAVES: Needles are four-sided (15-22 mm long), stiff, tips pointed but not sharp, green to bluish-green; crushed young needles smell camphor-like.

SEED CONE: Cylinder shaped, 3-6 cm long; outer edges rounded and smooth.

WOOD: Soft, light, clear grained; light colour; important commercial tree in northern BC.

FIRST PEOPLES: Roots used to weave coiled baskets by the Tsilhqot'in and other Interior Peoples; they also sew seams on birch bark containers; the hardened pitch makes a good chewing gum; spruce boughs can be used to make tea.

TREE FACTS: Seeds important food source for squirrels; difficult at times to distinguish from Englemann spruce; sometimes the 2 trees mate to produce a "hybrid" (half and half Englemann-white spruce tree).

black spruce

(Picea mariana (Mill.) BSP

APPEARANCE: Small tree up to 18 m; distinct narrow irregular crown – red squirrels chew off the tips of cone-bearing branches and the top resembles a "crows nest." When lower branches touch the forest floor they are able to grow roots (called layering) and sprout a new tree.

OCCURRENCE: Northern half of BC, east of Coast Mountains; common in swamps and bogs at southern end of range becoming more widespread in northeastern BC; extends southward to Smithers, Fraser Lake and Quesnel into north Thompson River to Blue River, isolated pockets in the Chilcotin.

BARK: Dark gray, scaly and similar to lodgepole pine.

LEAVES: Needles are four-sided (8-15 mm long), straight, blunt-pointed, dull grayish-green.

SEED CONE: Oval shaped, 2-3 cm long – smallest of all BC spruces; cones remain on trees for up to 30 years with viable seeds released gradually (quickly after a forest fire).

WOOD: Light, soft, fine grained; pale in colour; used for facial tissues and paper products.

FIRST PEOPLES: Pitch (spruce sap) chewed for pleasure and used for caulking or sealing the cracks of baskets and canoes.

TREE FACTS: *mariana* comes from Maryland, noting the widespread range of this tree species (although it does not exist in that state); steeped young black spruce shoots can be added to homebrew giving it a sharp tangy flavour.

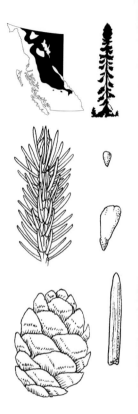

(Picea engelmannii Parry ex Englem.)

Engelmann spruce

APPEARANCE: From gnarled, stunted trees to 55 m high; from ragged, irregular to exquisite spire-crowns of stands in southern BC; lower branches often sloping downward bushy; can live for about 1000 years.

OCCURRENCE: Widespread in southeastern half of BC extending across the Rockies; subalpine tree growing from 1100 m up to the treeline, replaced by white spruce in northern half of the province; however Englemann is found in Skeena and Omineca Mountains and southward on westerly side of Coast Mountains; often hybridizes with white spruce.

BARK: Thin, loose grayish scales separated with brownish or rusty hues.

LEAVES: Needles are 4 sided (15-25 mm long), somewhat flexible, tip pointed or blunt, bluish-green often with white powder cover; crushed leaves aromatic.

SEED CONE: Cylinder shaped, 3-7 cm long; outer edges ragged towards the tip.

WOOD: Soft, straight grained; creamy white in colour; very important BC commercial timber.

FIRST PEOPLES: Split roots used for sewing baskets and bark canoes; pitch (spruce sap) used to treat sores and slivers; fresh needles chewed to treat coughs and made into tea.

TREE FACTS: Named after botanist George Engelmann (1809-84); excellent wood for making pianos, violins and other string instruments.

Sitka spruce

(Picea sitchensis (Bong.) Carrière

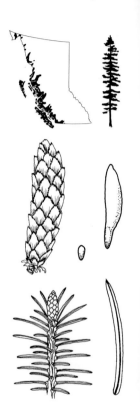

APPEARANCE: Very tall trees up to 95 m high; massive trunks, flaring buttresses at bases, open crown with horizontal branching, can live for about 850 years.

OCCURRENCE: Seldom found more than 80 kms from coastal (tidewater) BC and on adjacent islands; inhabits valley bottoms; scattered sightings reported in Fraser Valley near Hope and eastwards along Hope-Princeton Highway to Sumallo Grove; northern inland reports at Garibaldi Station and Cheakamus River valley.

BARK: Thin, large loose plate-like rusty-brown scales.

LEAVES: Flat (20-30 mm long), sharp-pointed; brisling outward in all direction from the twig.

SEED CONES: Cylinder-shaped (5-10 cm long), easily distinguishable by thin irregular wavy edges.

WOOD: Soft, straight grained, strong; creamy to pinkish brown in colour; excellent construction wood.

FIRST PEOPLES: Pliable roots and branches used to weave beautiful baskets and hats by Haida and Tlingit; inner bark and cambium is edible; pitch used for glue and caulking, and to make a medicinal salve; needled twigs make a tasty bush tea.

TREE FACTS: The unusually light yet strong wood was used for building aircraft's in both World Wars; *sitchensis* is from the Latin of Sitka Sound, Alaska; Sitka weevils (beetles) attack seedlings, therefore Sitka spruce infrequently replanted as commercial species on cut-over sites.

Tsuga heterophylla (Raf.) Sarg.)   **western hemlock**

APPEARANCE: Very tall tree up to 70 m high; narrow crown; drooping leader; sweeping horizontal branches with delicate, feather-like leaves; can live for more than 500 years.

OCCURRENCE: Common along coastal BC and in the interior "wet belt" cedar-hemlock forests, from low to mid elevations (up to 1500 m).

BARK: Smooth and reddish-brown when young; with age it darkens and develops furrows and scaly ridges; bark very high in tannin.

LEAVES: Flat, lengths vary (5-20 mm long); needles arranged in uneven 2 ranks.

SEED CONE: Oval-shaped (20-25 mm long); golden brown; tip rounded.

WOOD: Strong, light and fairly hard; whitish to light tan; important commercial tree in BC.

FIRST PEOPLES: Inner bark harvested in large quantities in the late spring and eaten fresh or dried and served with highbush cranberries and oulachen (fish) grease; tips of branches nibbled by hikers as a hunger suppressant; fresh needles for tea; the needled branches anchored in the ocean during herring spawning season to catch the herring eggs, a favourite food; the eggs are peeled off the needles, which give them a nice taste; bark for making dye and tanning materials; numerous parts of the tree provided medicines.

TREE FACTS: Drooping tree top is recognizable from a distance; *heterophylla* (from Latin) means variable leaves.

mountain hemlock

(Tsuga mertensiana (Bong.) Carrie

APPEARANCE: A tree that ranges in height from 15 to 55 m (usually 15 m); leader droops only slightly; branches have upward sweep at tips; can live for about 800 years.

OCCURRENCE: Common along coast of BC and near western hemlock but at higher elevations from about 700 m up to the treeline; found also in the interior "wet belt" near Revelstoke and Slocan Valley.

BARK: Thin and rough when young; with age it thickens, hardens, browns and develops narrow ridges.

LEAVES: Needles equal in length (1-3 cm long); all directions around the branch in disorderly fashion.

SEED CONE: Oblong-shaped (2.5-6 cm long); purplish-brown when ripe; at least two times longer than western hemlock.

WOOD: Strong, light and fairly hard; light reddish-brown; commercial timber.

FIRST PEOPLES: The inner bark and cambium are edible.

TREE FACTS: Named "tree-mother" after Japanese *Tsuga*; can tolerate snow packs as deep as 6 m; soils rarely freeze in the subalpine and mountain hemlock roots can grow at near-freezing soil temperatures (0.5 °C).

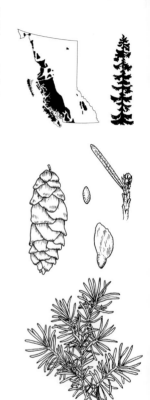

(Pseudotsuga menziesii (Mirb.) Franco var. menziesii)

coastal Douglas-fir

APPEARANCE: A very tall tree of up to 93 m; crown of younger trees are pyramidal, sweeping branches with tips curved upwards; older trees lose this form, have crooked branches with flattened or irregular tops; can live for over 1000 years.

OCCURRENCE: Southern coastal half of the province, found in valley bottoms and up to about 850 m.

BARK: Thin, smooth, gray with resin blisters when young; with age becomes very thick (excellent protection from surface fire), rough and dark brown, ridged with reddish-brown tinges.

LEAVES: Needles are flat (2-3 cm long), yellow-green; sharp pointed but not as prickly as spruce; smells of apples when crushed.

SEED CONE: Oval-shaped (5-10 cm long); yellowish-brown to purplish-brown; three-pronged tail-like "bracts" are distinct features.

WOOD: Hard, exceptionally strong; reddish brown to yellowish white; important commercial timber.

FIRST PEOPLES: Wood used for making various implements from harpoon shafts to dipnet hoops and handles; pitch used for caulking canoes, sealing joints and medicinally for treating wounds and skin irritations; the bark is an excellent fuel.

TREE FACTS: Named after the explorer-botanist David Douglas; Latin - *Pseudo* false *tsuga* hemlock; hyphen between Douglas and fir denotes that this tree is not a "true fir" or *Abies*.

interior Douglas-fir

(Pseudotsuga menziesii var. glauca (Beissn.) Franco)

APPEARANCE: A tall tree up to about 55 m; crown of younger trees are pyramidal shaped, sweeping branches with tips curved upwards; older trees lose this form, developing crooked branches with flattened or irregular tops; trees can live for over 700 years.

OCCURRENCE: Valley bottoms and up to about 1075 m in interior BC and up to 1800 m in the Rockies; occurs as far north as Stuart and McLeod Lakes.

BARK: Thin, smooth, gray-brown with resin blisters when young; with age becomes very thick (excellent protection from surface fire), rough, corky and dark brown, ridged with reddish-brown tinges.

LEAVES: Needles are flat (2-3 cm long), yellow-green or blue-green; sharp pointed but not as prickly as spruce; smells of apples when crushed.

SEED CONE: Oval-egg-shaped (4-7.5 cm long); yellowish-brown to purplish-brown; three-pronged tail-like "bracts" are distinct features.

WOOD: Hard, exceptionally strong; reddish brown to yellowish white; important commercial timber.

FIRST PEOPLES: Under some conditions (hot, dry summer; moist soil) interior Douglas-fir produces a crystalline sugar (from around wounds and old fire scars), which was a treat whenever it was found; the young twigs can be made into tea; the pitch is used for a medicinal salve; green branches used in sweat-baths and other ceremonial functions.

TREE FACTS: Interior Douglas-fir looks "bluer" than the coastal variety because of the wax covering its needles; *Pseudotsuga* grows in North America, Japan and China.

(Abies lasiocarpa (Hook.) Nutt.)* **subalpine fir**

APPEARANCE: A tall tree up to 50 m (but usually 20-35 m tall); crown is slender with spire-like top, short drooping branches, some touch the ground; trees can live for about 400 years.

OCCURRENCE: Throughout the province except for the Haida Gwaii; subalpine areas; most common east of the Coast Mountains above 600 m on the interior plateau and continues to timberline.

BARK: Smooth; ash-gray and covered with raised resin blisters when young; thickens with age becoming gray-brown and scaly.

LEAVES: Needles even, flat (2.5-4 cm long); grayish-green to light bluish-green; curving upwards from side of twig and standing upright; uniquely aromatic when crushed.

SEED CONE: Barrel-shaped (4-10 cm long), upright; grayish-brown; deciduous in September, leaving a bare central axis.

WOOD: Light, even grained; whitish to yellow brown in colour; commercially important timber.

FIRST PEOPLES: Known as the "medicine tree" in some interior Salish languages; boughs are used as a scent to mask human odour for hunters and others in the woods, and to make a sleeping mattress; tea made from the bark used for coughs; the needles are used as an incense.

TREE FACTS: *Abies* from the Latin *abeo* meaning "to rise" referring to tree height; *lasiocarpa* from Greek *lasio* "shaggy" or "hairy" and *carpos* "a fruit," referring to disintegrating mature cones.

57

amabilis fir or Pacific silver fir

(Abies amabilis (Dougl. ex Loud.) Dougl. ex J. Forbes)

APPEARANCE: A tall tree of about 55 m; crown is slender with spire-like top, short drooping branches, some touch the ground; trees can live for about 450 years.

OCCURRENCE: Western slopes of the Coast Mountains and on Vancouver Island; from sea level in Douglas-fir-hemlock forests and subalpine in mountain hemlock-yellow cedar forests.

BARK: Smooth; light gray, covered with raised resin blisters when young; thickens with age becoming scaly, grooved at the base of old trees.

LEAVES: Needles even with short central row, flat (2-3 cm long); dark green, 2 distinct white lines on underside; spread horizontally and cover the top-side of branch; when crushed, smell like ripe strawberries.

SEED CONE: Barrel-shaped (9-14 cm long); upright, brown; deciduous in September, leaving a bare central axis.

WOOD: Light; soft; and yellowish brown; timber important commercially.

FIRST PEOPLES: Fragrant boughs used for floor coverings and bedding; liquid pitch from bark blisters used to make a medicinal salve.

TREE FACTS: Called "silver fir" because of the shining silvery undersides of the needles; *amabilis* from Latin meaning "lovely"; boughs used for Christmas wreaths; sometimes also called "balsam fir."

(Abies grandis (Dougl. ex D. Don) Lindl.)

grand fir

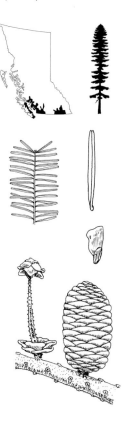

APPEARANCE: A very tall tree up to about 80 m (coast) and 55 m (interior); crown is pyramid-shaped when young; with age, the tops become rounder, lower branches extend gracefully like a skirt; can live for about 300 years.

OCCURRENCE: Lower slopes up to about 900 m and valleys of southern coastal region and Vancouver Island; from Bute Inlet southwards to Victoria, extending northwards along the Fraser River to Boston Bar; southern interior in Kootenay and Arrow Lakes region.

BARK: Smooth; grayish-brown; covered with raised resin blisters and white blotches when young; becomes deep brown, thickens, scaly, forms dark gray flat ridges with age.

LEAVES: Needles, flat (3-5 cm long); dark green with 2 distinct white lines on underside, even horizontally spreading; crushed needles are very aromatic, with citrus smell.

SEED CONE: Barrel-shaped (5-12 cm long); upright, green to purplish; deciduous in September, leaving a bare central axis; produces least seed of British Columbian *Abies*.

WOOD: Light, soft; and light brown; used for saw timber and pulp.

FIRST PEOPLES: Bark and boughs used to make a medicinal tea for colds and flu.

TREE FACTS: Botanist David Douglas named this tree "grand" for its noteworthy height and diameter; resin popped from blisters from the bark, treat insect bites and small cuts.

western redcedar

(Thuja plicata Donn ex D. Do▪

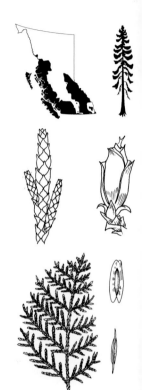

APPEARANCE: A tall tree up to about 60 m; full crown, symmetrical when young, branches spreading or slightly droopy with upward turn; with age long irregular branches, base of trees fluted with buttress; can live for well over 1000 years.

OCCURRENCE: Common west of Coast Mountains, grows in valley bottoms and up to 875 m; interior wet belt up to elevations of 1300 m; along rivers in Smilkameen, Okanagan, Columbia and Kootenay valley bottoms.

BARK: Thin and stringy; reddish-brown; shiny when young; shredded and forming narrow flat ridges with age.

LEAVES: Scaly (1-2 mm long); scales lie in pairs pressed to twig; yellowish-green.

SEED CONE: Small egg-shaped (1-2 cm long); clustered, upright, green becoming brown and woody; cones open in September, over winter on tree.

WOOD: Very light, soft; straight grained; rot resistant; shingles, shakes, fences, decks and poles; prized commercial timber.

FIRST PEOPLES: Bark used for baskets, clothes and mats; roots and branches used for baskets and rope; wood for houses, totem poles, dugout canoes, bentwood boxes, paddles, ceremonial drums and many other important day to day implements; called "the cornerstone of Northwest Coast Aboriginal culture."

TREE FACTS: Western redcedar is BCs provincial tree; its red wood is extremely rot resistant because of a chemical called "thujaplicin"; great source of kindling for starting camping fires.

(Chamaecyparis nootkatensis
(D. Don) Spach)

yellow cedar

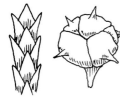

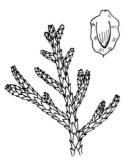

APPEARANCE: A tall tree up to 50 m; trunk twisted and tapers toward top, long sweeping drooping branches; treetops droop like hemlocks; wood and branches have a distinct pungent smell.

OCCURRENCE: Mid to high elevations along coastal SW BC with mountain hemlock and amabilis fir (found occasionally at sea level: west coast of Vancouver Island, north coast) up to Alaska; pockets in Slocan Valley, West Kootenays; can live for more than 1600 years.

BARK: Smooth, reddish bark when young; dirty-white to grayish brown; stringy and brittle with age.

LEAVES: Scaly (2-3 mm long), alternating pairs up to 4 rows on a twig; dull bluish-green.

SEED CONE: Small berry-like (about 5 mm long); mature scales are triangular and upright, green with purple tinge, cones mature in second year with a big crop occurring every 5 years.

WOOD: Light, hard, strong, narrow grained; pale yellow; pungent odor; very rot resistant; prized commercial timber.

FIRST PEOPLES: Wood used to make paddles and other items; soft inner bark used for clothing, hats, and blankets.

TREE FACTS: Also called yellow cypress; amazingly, relatively free of any major insects or diseases; (noot-kuh-ten-sehs) for Nootka sound, west coast of Vancouver Island.

Rocky Mountain juniper

(Juniperus scopulorum Sarg.)*

APPEARANCE: Small tree up to 20 m, slender crown with drooping branches also found as bush and bushy-like tree.

OCCURRENCE: Low to mid elevation dry forests; southern half of the province; east of Coast Mountains to Rocky Mountain trench; occasional trees found in north-central BC, along eastern side of Vancouver Island.

BARK: Thin, stringy and reddish brown.

LEAVES: Pointy, sharp, needle-like leaves (15 mm long) when young; with age, smooth, scale-like (similar to western redcedar), pale yellowish-green to whitish-green.

SEED CONE: Berry-like (up to 7.5 mm wide), bluish purple with white powdery coating, fragrant; 2 years to ripen, contains 1 to 2 seeds.

WOOD: Moderately heavy, hard, narrow grained: very aromatic, reddish heart wood with a wide white ring of sapwood; very rot resistant.

FIRST PEOPLES: Boughs used as a fumigant and incense; air freshener in sweat-houses, and as a protective wash; tough wood used for bows and digging sticks, and as fuel for smoking hides.

TREE FACTS: Juniper berries are used to make gin; its aromatic wood makes excellent cedar-closets; *scopulorum* (of rocks or cliffs) where it is found.

(Taxus brevifolia Nutt.)* **Pacific yew**

APPEARANCE: A small tree up to 20 m; trunk twisted, thrives in the shade and its branches are of irregular lengths; can live for hundreds of years.

OCCURRENCE: Low elevations (near sea level) on coast; up to 1150 m in the interior ranges of Cariboo, Monashee, Selkirk and Purcell Mountains.

BARK: Thin, stringy and scaly; dark reddish brown to reddish-purple.

LEAVES: Flat, needle-like leaves (15 - 30 mm long); pointy tips, short stems; intense dull green.

SEED CONE: Berry-like and called and "aril" (up to 8 mm wide), male and female cones on separate trees; greenish berries that turn red in September; aril contains 1 seed.

WOOD: Heavy, hard, strong, narrow grained; reddish to dark orange with yellow sapwood; decay resistant.

FIRST PEOPLES: Durable wood was prized by coastal and interior tribes; used to makes bows, clubs, wedges, spears and digging sticks; young wood used for snowshoe rims; bark and wood used traditionally for medicine.

TREE FACTS: The medicine "taxol" comes from the yew tree, it's used to combat breast, ovarian and lung cancers, AIDS and heart disease; yew seeds and needles are poisonous to humans; many different birds eat the fleshy arils and disperse the seeds.

THE BROADLEAVES

Rhamnus purshiana DC.)

casacara

APPEARANCE: A small tree up to 20 m; young trees have slender trunks becoming twisted and irregular limbed with age; distinct winter buds that do not close completely.

OCCURRENCE: Low elevations on Vancouver Island and Gulf Islands; mainland up to Bella Coola; southern interior in wet cedar-hemlock forest around Arrow and Kootenay Lakes, Adams River, east of Creston to Yahk.

BARK: Thin, smooth; silver gray and scaly at the base of older trees.

LEAVES: Alternate, deciduous, oval-shaped, 5-15 cm long, finely toothed.

FLOWERS: Greenish-yellow flowers occurring in the springtime.

FRUITS: Blue-black berries, rounded, 8-13 mm across, found in clusters; edible but not great tasting.

WOOD: Light, narrow grained, brittle; brown tinge to red; non commercial timber.

FIRST PEOPLES: Bark well known as a laxative; made into a medicinal tea, which was also drunk as a tonic and for headaches; traditionally only a strip of bark would be taken from a tree, allowing the tree to heal; wood used for D-adze handles.

TREE FACTS: The wood and bark of this tree contain a drug, "cascara sagrada," used as a laxative; during World War II it was over-harvested so extensively that the government had to legislate its protection; the drug is now made synthetically.

black hawthorn

(Crataegus douglasii Lindl*.*

APPEARANCE: A small tree up to 15 m; needle-sharp spines (1.5-3 cm long) on branches.

OCCURRENCE: Throughout the lower 2/3 of the province at low to mid elevations, along edges of streams and meadows.

BARK: Rough, scaly, grayish with patches of lichen; similar to Pacific crabapple.

LEAVES: Alternate, deciduous, thick, oval-shaped with 5 to 9 lobes at the top end.

FLOWERS: White, smelly; saucer-shaped blossoms occurring in April and May.

FRUITS: Blackish-purple little apples about 1.5 cm long, found in bunches, large seeds, apples edible by late July; important food source for birds.

WOOD: Hard, narrow grained; non commercial timber.

FIRST PEOPLES: Thorns used for fish hooks, game pieces, for lancing skin blisters. Charcoal used to make face paint; tough wood used for digging sticks.

TREE FACTS: *Crataegus* is from classical Greek *kratos* (strength) after its strong wood properties; "haguthorn" from Anglo-Saxon is "fence with thorns."

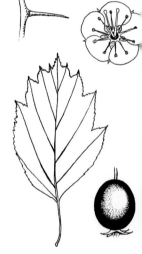

(Arbutus menziesii Pursh)

Arbutus or Pacific madrone

APPEARANCE: A medium tree up to 30 m; twisted crooked trunk with irregular crown; can live up to 200 years.

OCCURRENCE: Confined to southeastern Vancouver Island and the Gulf Islands at sea level; found growing in Garry oak communities; sea level on mainland, restricted to coast from Bute Inlet southwards.

BARK: Thin, smooth, green when young, becoming thicker with age, reddish orange, peeling in flakes or strips; only native BC tree that exhibits this beautiful colouration.

LEAVES: Alternate, evergreen, 7.5-15 cm long with a thick leather-like texture.

FLOWERS: Creamy white, bell-shaped fragrant flowers occurring in early April.

FRUITS: Orange-red berries about 9 mm across; very important food source for robins and thrushes during the winter months.

WOOD: Heavy, hard, brownish; non commercial timber.

FIRST PEOPLES: Bark and leaves used medicinally for treating colds. In a Saanich story, this tree anchored people in their canoes to the top of the mountain during the Great Flood.

TREE FACTS: Arbutus is from the Latin for "strawberry" for its bright red fruits; it is the only native evergreen broadleaf tree in Canada.

bitter cherry

(Prunus emarginata Dougl.)

APPEARANCE: Medium tree up to 25 m tall; slender trunk, branches relatively straight and pointing upwards.

OCCURRENCE: From sea level to about 850 m on Vancouver Island and south coast, found in cedar-hemlock forests of southern interior and into subalpine.

BARK: Thin, reddish-brown on young trees; horizontal rows of raised lenticels, grayish-brown on older trees.

LEAVES: Alternate, deciduous, oval (4-8 cm long), fine rounded teeth.

FLOWERS: White or pink, pungent, in bunches of 5-12 and occurring in April or May.

FRUITS: Pea-sized bright red cherries, stems about 1.5 cm long, ripen in July or August; taste extremely bitter.

WOOD: Light, brittle; used as fuel wood or ornamentally.

FIRST PEOPLES: Tough, stringy bark used for wrapping joints on harpoons and arrows, and hafts of bows; also for decorating cedar-root coiled baskets; bark can be dyed black by burying it in swampy ground for several weeks, or soaking in water with rusty nails.

TREE FACTS: *Prunus* is Latin for "plum" tree and from Greek *prunos* (plum).

Prunus virginiana var. *demissa* (Nutt.) Torr.

choke cherry

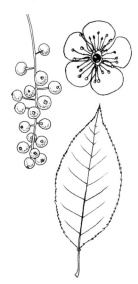

APPEARANCE: Small tree up to 9 m in height, often multi stemmed.

OCCURRENCE: East of the Coast Mountains but found occasionally on southern Vancouver Island and in the Fraser delta; extends into the north country and is associated with poison ivy.

BARK: Grayish-brown to black and covered with many small lenticels.

LEAVES: Alternate, deciduous, dark green, rounded at base, finely toothed.

FLOWERS: White, clustered at the end of branches in May.

FRUITS: Red to dark purple berries (0.5-1.5 cm across), irregular stem lengths.

WOOD: Light, narrow grained, brittle; non commercial timber.

FIRST PEOPLES: Cherries are a major food source in the Interior; dried and pounded for winter; still harvested and made into syrup and juice concentrate; wood used for handles and decorative purposes; bark used in medicinal tonic.

TREE FACTS: Bruised bark gives off a sweet almond smell but has a bitter taste due to cyanide; cherries make excellent jellies and syrups.

NOTE: Seeds, bark and leaves of cherries produce cyanide and can be toxic.

pin cherry

(Prunus pensylvanica L. f.)

APPEARANCE: Small tree up about 13 m in height, trunk slender and relatively straight, narrow crown with rounded top; trees can live for about 50 years.

OCCURRENCE: Interior southern half of the province with some isolated occurrences elsewhere.

BARK: Dark reddish-brown, shiny when young and covered in orange lenticels; mature bark has horizontal-like papery strips with large lenticels.

LEAVES: Alternate, deciduous, slender, tapering to sharp point; turns bright purplish-red in autumn.

FLOWERS: White, clusters of 4-7, occur mid May to early June.

FRUITS: Bright red (6-8 mm in diameter) and about 6 mm long, ripens in August and early September; important source of food for many birds.

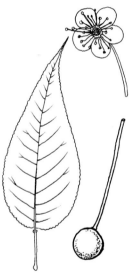

WOOD: Light, narrow grained, brittle; non commercial timber.

FIRST PEOPLES: Fruits eaten; bark strips used to decorate cedar-root and spruce-root baskets.

TREE FACTS: Its stones contain toxic cyanide but fleshy fruit is edible.

Malus fusca (Raf.) C.K. Schneid.)

Pacific crabapple

APPEARANCE: A small tree up to 20 m, bushy when open grown, looks to have thorns but upon closer inspection has only sharp spurs.

OCCURRENCE: Along the entire coast of BC in moist areas such as stream beds and swamps; from sea level to mid elevations.

BARK: Dark, furrowed, scaly; contains cyanide producing compounds.

LEAVES: Alternate, deciduous, dark green, irregular lobes, sharp toothed, prominent veins.

FLOWERS: White and pink, fragrant, in clusters (about 2-3 cm across), occur in May.

FRUITS: Purplish-red to yellowish, oblong apples (about 1.5-2 cm long); edible but tart tasting.

WOOD: Hard, light brown, narrow-grained; wood is turned for ornamental purposes.

FIRST PEOPLES: Fruits are an important source of food for Coastal Peoples; usually stored for winter in containers with water and oil; whipped with oulachen (fish) grease into a favourite dessert. Tough wood used for adze handles and digging sticks; bark used medicinally.

TREE FACTS: The apples are an important source of winter food for purple finches, grouse and other birds.

red alder

(Alnus rubra Bong.)

APPEARANCE: A medium sized tree up to 35 m; straight limbs, conical crown; lives for about 75 years.

OCCURRENCE: Coastal, very common west of the Coast Mountains up to Alaska; low to mid elevations.

BARK: Light gray; older trees exhibit blotchy white lichen markings with irregular flat plates.

LEAVES: Alternate, deciduous, oval (7-14 cm long), dull-toothed forming rounded lobes (unlike other 3 native alders), outer edge of leaf curls under, straight veins run to leaf margin.

FLOWERS: Male pollen catkins (droopy looking tails) occur in May, female cone-like seed catkin (upright at the end of the twigs) before leaves appear.

FRUITS: Mature seed catkins 1.5-3 cm long, release winged seeds in September and onwards.

WOOD: Light, fine grained, light brown, turns red after cutting; used for furniture industry.

FIRST PEOPLES: Wood used as fuel for smoking salmon, and for carving dishes, spoons and masks; inner bark eaten in springtime; bark used to make a reddish dye for cedar-bark and other materials; also an important medicine for skin infections and respiratory ailments.

TREE FACTS: It takes nitrogen from the air and "fixes-it" (a chemical process) in its tree root nodules (this tree makes the soil very fertile); "alder" from Old English meaning "reddish-yellow" when the wood is exposed to air.

**(*Alnus viridis* ssp. *sinuata*
(Regel) Á. Löve & D. Löve)**

Sitka alder

APPEARANCE: A small tree up to 15 m; slender trunk or sometimes multi stemmed, branches reach outwards forming a ragged outline; also found in avalanche shoots where stems often bend down the slope before rising (caused by the force of snow sliding down the avalanche path).

OCCURRENCE: Throughout BC except in northeast corner, occurring on mountain slopes above 750 m, occasionally but not often at lower elevations, common in avalanche shoots.

BARK: Reddish-gray green, smooth, long horizontal lenticels; trees in wetter areas are covered in a scaly greenish white lichen.

LEAVES: Alternate, deciduous, 1.5-7.5 cm long, broad lobes, wavy edges, sharp teeth.

FLOWERS: Pollen (male) and seed (female) catkins appear at the same time as leaves.

FRUITS: Mature seed catkins 1-2 cm long, found in clusters of 3-6, seeds have wide wings.

WOOD: Light, soft, flexible; non commercial timber.

FIRST PEOPLES: Bark use as a reddish-coloured dye, like red alder; wood used for spoons and other small items.

TREE FACTS: Alder leaves do not turn brown before leaf fall in the autumn.

mountain alder

(Alnus tenuifolia Nutt.)

APPEARANCE: Small tree up to 20 m; conical crown with branches pointing upwards.

OCCURRENCE: East of Coast Mountains and northward to Yukon; ranges from valley bottoms to subalpine; grows with Sitka alder.

BARK: Gray to reddish gray, older trees flakey and scaly near the base with greenish white lichens.

LEAVES: Alternate, deciduous, dark green, 5-10 cm long, double toothed, sharp teeth.

FLOWERS: Pollen catkins (male) 1.5-2.5 cm long, immature female catkins 2-4 mm long.

FRUITS: Clusters of 2-5 mature seed catkins (9-13 mm long), narrow winged seeds, female catkins mature in late summer.

WOOD: Light, soft, similar to Sitka alder, but decays quickly; non commercial timber.

FIRST PEOPLES: Wood used for smoking meats and fish, and bark as a dye for tanning hides.

TREE FACTS: The bark contains "salicin," a potent medicine used to combat rheumatic fever.

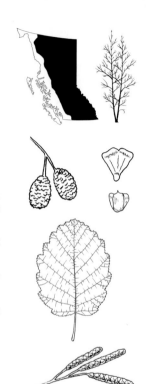

(Alnus rugosa (Du Roi) Spreng.)　　　　　　　　**speckled alder**

APPEARANCE: Small tree up to 10 m, crooked trunk often multi stemmed.

OCCURRENCE: Northeast corner of the province, low elevations along stream edges and swamps, grows with black spruces.

BARK: Smooth, reddish-brown with large horizontal lenticels.

LEAVES: Alternate, deciduous, dull green, 5-10 cm long, double toothed, sheds leaves early in the autumn.

FLOWERS: Pollen (male) catkins (droopy looking tails) 5-8 cm, immature seed (female) catkins (upright at the end of the twigs) 2-5 mm long and visible during the winter.

FRUITS: Mature seed catkins are 10-17 mm long, clusters of 2-4; narrow winged seeds.

WOOD: Light, soft; non commercial timber.

FIRST PEOPLES: Bark used for reddish dye, like the other alders.

TREE FACTS: Alder and birch are closely related: each have very small winged seeds.

white birch

(Betula papyrifera **Marsh.**)

APPEARANCE: Medium tree up to 35 m in height; slender trunk, oval shaped crown; trees can live over 150 years.

OCCURRENCE: Common throughout most of the province; noticeably absent from Haida Gwaii, Vancouver Island and along coastal wet mainland.

BARK: Thin, smooth, reddish brown on young trees becoming creamy white with age and shedding in thin sheets, very distinctive feature.

LEAVES: Alternate, deciduous, dull green, 5-10 cm long, triangular, pointed tip, double toothed.

FLOWERS: Male pollen catkins (droopy looking tails) in clusters of 1-3, 9.5 cm long at pollination, seed (female) catkins (upright at the end of the twigs), 1-2 cm long and pink or red.

FRUITS: Mature seed catkins 3-6 cm long, ripen in September, deciduous, bare axis left.

WOOD: Strong, pale, burns at high heat; commercially used for furniture and flooring.

FIRST PEOPLES: Bark peeled off standing trees in early summer and used to make a wide variety of vessels and containers, as well as baby cradles and canoes. Careful harvesting removes only the outer layer; inner bark hardens and protects the tree, keeping it alive; papery shreds of bark used as tinder; wood used as fuel and for carving spoons and masks.

TREE FACTS: Birch resin contains "zylitol" and is used as a natural tooth cleaner; birch bark can be used to start a camping fire even if it is soaking wet.

(Betula occidentalis Hook.)

water birch or western birch

APPEARANCE: A small tree reaching a height of about 14 m; open crown with upright branches drooping at the tips.

OCCURRENCE: East of Coast Mountains to the Rocky Mountains, grows along streams with poplars, willows and alders.

BARK: Thin, reddish to purplish brown, shiny, prominent horizontal lenticels, does not peel readily.

LEAVES: Alternate, deciduous, oval shaped, 2-5 cm long, double toothed sharp edges.

FLOWERS: Male pollen catkins (droopy looking tails) 6 cm long, seed (female) catkins 2 cm long.

FRUITS: Mature seed catkins 2.5-4.5 cm long, mature in late August, deciduous, bare axis left.

WOOD: Narrow grained, light, soft; locally used as fence posts and fuel wood.

FIRST PEOPLES: Flexible twigs used to make baby cradles and baskets.

TREE FACTS: In the springtime birch sap is used to make syrup; important wildlife habitat tree.

Alaska paper birch

(Betula neoalaskana Sarg.)

APPEARANCE: A small tree up to 9 m; narrow crown with upright branches and some drooping at the tips.

OCCURRENCE: Northeast of the province extending from Peace River area north to Fort Nelson; low elevations in bogs and poorly drained soil, grows along side of black spruce.

BARK: Thin, smooth, reddish brown when young becoming creamy white with age; peels off in thin layers (similar to paper birch).

LEAVES: Alternate, deciduous, triangular shaped, shiny dark green, 4-7 cm long.

FLOWERS: Pollen (male) catkins (droopy looking tails) 2-4.5 cm long, seed (female) catkins (upright at the end of the twigs) 1-2.5 cm long.

FRUITS: Mature seed catkins 2.5-4.5 cm long, ripens in late August; seeds with large wings, deciduous, bare axis left.

WOOD: Narrow grained, light, soft; locally used as fuel wood.

FIRST PEOPLES: Strong inner bark (with its watertight properties) used for canoes, baskets, dishes, snow goggles, moose calls and toboggans; sap can be used as a sweet beverage and syrup.

TREE FACTS: In Roman Britain, clay pots were glued together using birch bark tar, which was distilled from its bark; *Betula* means "pitch."

(Populus balsamifera ssp. trichocarpa (Torr. & A. Gray) Brayshaw)

black cottonwood

APPEARANCE: A tall tree up to 55 m; long straight trunk, narrow crown; can live for about 175 years.

OCCURRENCE: Widespread throughout the province and southern half of Vancouver Island, uncommon on Haida Gwaii or on the outer coast; mid to lower elevations along streams.

BARK: Smooth, greenish when young becoming gray brown and furrowed with age.

LEAVES: Alternate, deciduous, widely triangular (6-13 cm long), dark green, rounded teeth.

FLOWERS: Pollen (male) catkins 4-6 cm long, seed (female) catkins 6-9 cm long.

FRUITS: Capsules on catkins 3-5 mm long, split into 3 parts and release tiny white seeds.

WOOD: Soft, lightweight; used for veneer, plywood and toilet paper.

FIRST PEOPLES: Sweet inner bark is eaten; sweet smelling resin from buds used to make a healing skin salve, and as medicine for coughs and colds; wood used to make dugout canoes in Interior; sheets of bark used to make buckets and to line food cache pits; inner bark sometimes spun with cedar-bark for nets; "cotton" from fruits used to stuff pillows and mattresses.

TREE FACTS: Named for the white hairs (on mature seed) that helps them float through the air and looks like "cotton"; bees collect resin (potent anti-infectant) from buds, use it in their hives to seal holes and prevent intruders.

balsam poplar

(Populus balsamifera L. ssp. *balsamifera)*

APPEARANCE: Medium sized tree up to 27 m; root suckering creates clonal poplars; individual trees can live for more than 150 years.

OCCURRENCE: Across northern BC from the upper Stikine River and Atlin, east to the Rocky Mountains.

BARK: Greenish-brown when young, becoming gray and furrowed with age.

LEAVES: Paler green not silvery like black cottonwood, otherwise very similar, but often more elongated. In the springtime, the resin on the unfolding leaves acts as an insecticide against the larvae of defoliating insects.

FLOWERS: Pollen (male) catkins 4-8 cm long, seed (female) catkins 8-20 cm long, male and female catkins on separate trees.

FRUITS: Mature capsule splits into 2 parts and release tiny white seeds (see black cottonwood).

WOOD: Weak, soft, whitish; used for pulpwood.

FIRST PEOPLES: Inner live bark (cambium) eaten in the springtime, boiled and served to children as worm medicine; large trees used to make dugout canoes.

TREE FACTS: Called "balsam poplar" because the sticky buds are full of a gummy resin that has an unmistakable sweet smell of "balsam"; useful for the construction of large stick nests as well as cavity nesting.

Populus tremuloides Michx.)

trembling aspen

APPEARANCE: Medium sized tree up to 27 m; long straight trunks, rounded crown; root suckering enables groves of aspens to prosper; individual trees can live for about 200 years.

OCCURRENCE: Widespread east of the Coast Mountains, from valley bottoms to the subalpine (1250 m), found in patches on east side of Vancouver Island and some Gulf Islands.

BARK: Smooth, green with white chalk-like bloom; black "horseshoe-like" markings.

LEAVES: Alternate, deciduous, heart-shaped, deep green, 4-8 cm long, fine teeth.

FLOWERS: Inconspicuous catkins appear early in spring before leaves.

FRUITS: Mature capsule splits into 2 parts, ripens 4-6 weeks after flowering, mast (large) seed crop every 4-5 years.

WOOD: Weak, soft, whitish; commercially important for pulpwood, waferboards, and chop-sticks.

FIRST PEOPLES: Wood used as fuel and for construction; whitish powder from bark used as talcum powder; bark and roots chewed and applied to stop bleeding.

TREE FACTS: Called "trembling aspen" because its leaves have flat stalks and "tremble" with the slightest wind; powdery white material on trunk is a natural sunscreen – protection against UV radiation; important wildlife tree especially for beavers.

Pacific willow

(Salix lucida ssp. lasiandra
(Benth.) E. Murr.)

APPEARANCE: A medium tree up to 25 m; crooked trunk with a number of upright limbs, it is the tallest native willow in BC; there are many other native willows in the province but they are considered bushes not trees.

OCCURRENCE: Widespread through the province along streams, rivers and wetlands in low and at mid elevations.

BARK: Gray brown to blackish, at the base darkening with age and becoming furrowed, young twigs are yellow and some branches are orange-brown.

LEAVES: Alternate, deciduous, lance-shaped, shiny dark green 5-13 cm long.

FLOWERS: Pollen (male) catkins 2-4.5 cm long, seed (female) catkins 4-7 cm long.

FRUITS: Mature smooth capsules 4-9 mm long, light reddish brown, seeds are fuzzy, tiny and white.

WOOD: Soft, pale, brown; non commercial timber.

FIRST PEOPLES: Used to make twine from bark and rope by twisting bark and twigs together; dead, dry wood and roots used for firedrills (making a fire using a rapidly-twirling stick of wood into another small piece of wood); used as a pain-killing and fever-reducing medicine.

TREE FACTS: *lucida* is from Latin and means "shiny" - named after its twigs; very important food source for moose during winter months. The painkiller acetyl salicylic acid (ASA) is named after *Salix* (willow), which is an original source of salicylic acid.

(Quercus garryana Dougl.)

Garry oak

APPEARANCE: Medium tree up to 30 m; when mature its silhouette is exquisite, gnarled limbs and indeed massive; can live for 300 years or more.

OCCURRENCE: Limited distribution, southern tip Vancouver Island along east coast up to Comox, common on Gulf Islands, several patches along Fraser River above Yale and on Sumas Mountain; often grows with Arbutus.

BARK: Light gray, with age it develops furrows and some scales.

LEAVES: Alternate, deciduous, dark green, 7-11 cm long, 5-7 lobes (very distinctive).

FLOWERS: Male and female flowers are tiny, separate on the same tree; flowers as the leaves appear.

FRUITS: Smooth, brown acorn 1.5-2.5 cm long, shed in the autumn sometimes with husks on.

WOOD: Hard, strong, heavy; non commercial timber.

FIRST PEOPLES: Acorns used as food, but have to be soaked in running water for a long time to leach out the bitter tannins.

TREE FACTS: David Douglas, botanist and explorer, named this tree after Nicholas Garry of the Hudson's Bay Co., for assistance he provided during his trips; *Quercus* is Latin for "oak"; only native oak to BC; Steller's Jays like to eat these acorns, and help to distribute the trees by burying the acorns in the ground and sometimes forgetting about them.

western flowering dogwood

(Cornus nuttallii Audub.
ex Torr. & Gray)

APPEARANCE: A medium tree up to 25 m; slightly tapered trunk, sometimes lopsided crown, with whorled branches.

OCCURRENCE: Restricted to SE BC, along eastern coast of Vancouver Island and adjacent mainland coast, into the Fraser Canyon northward beyond Hope; low elevation species.

BARK: Thin, gray, becoming dark brown with ridges and plates as ages.

LEAVES: Opposite, deciduous, 8-15 cm long, widest near the middle, tapers at both ends, edges are wavy.

FLOWERS: 6-13 cm across; dense greenish button-like cluster, surrounded by 5-6 showy, white bracts.

FRUITS: Compact (20-30), bead-like, red berry-like (10-13 mm long), mature in August and September.

WOOD: Narrow grained, hard; not legally allowed to cut wood.

FIRST PEOPLES: Wood used for bows, arrows and tool handles, bark boiled to make blackish dye and also used medicinally; fruits used to treat acne.

TREE FACTS: Provincial flower of BC – trees protected by law from harvesting; pileated woodpeckers, flickers and band-tailed pigeons are but a few of the birds that eat the dogwood fruits.

(Acer macrophyllum Pursh)

bigleaf maple

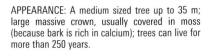

APPEARANCE: A medium sized tree up to 35 m; large massive crown, usually covered in moss (because bark is rich in calcium); trees can live for more than 250 years.

OCCURRENCE: West of Coast Mountains at low elevations, Vancouver northwards to Bella Coola, into Fraser Canyon up to Boston Bar, just east of Hope along Hope-Princeton Highway.

BARK: Green on younger trees becoming grayish-brown with furrows and narrow ridges.

LEAVES: Opposite, deciduous, shiny dark green, huge leaf (up to 40 cm long), 5 lobes.

FLOWERS: Small, greenish-yellow, fragrant, flowers drooping in clusters; male and female flowers in same cluster.

FRUITS: Wings 30-45 mm long, seed case hairy, mature in late August.

WOOD: Fine grained, moderately hard; commercially used for furniture, cabinets, floors.

FIRST PEOPLES: The even-grained, hard wood valued for making paddles; called "paddle tree" in some Coast Salish languages; also used for spindle whorls; inner bark used to make soapberry whippers; bark used medicinally.

TREE FACTS: Has largest native leaf-size in Canada; hence Greek *makros* (large) and *phyllon* (leaf); bees make delicious honey from bigleaf maple flowers.

Douglas or Rocky Mountain maple

(Acer glabrum Torr. var. *douglasii* (Hook.) Dippel)

APPEARANCE: A medium tree up to 25 m; short trunk, sometimes multi stemmed, irregular crown.

OCCURRENCE: Widespread east of Coast Mountains in lower 2/3 of BC, grows in valley bottoms up to about 1250 m.

BARK: Thin, smooth, pale green to dull brown.

LEAVES: Opposite, deciduous, dark green, 7-14 cm long, 3-5 lobes, coarse teeth; lovely shades of red in the autumn.

FLOWERS: Yellowish-green with 5 petals (about 5 mm across).

FRUITS: Wings 18-24 mm long, seed case strongly wrinkled, mature in midsummer.

WOOD: Hard, tough; not commercially used.

FIRST PEOPLES: Wood used for snowshoe frames, small bowls, paddles and ceremonial rattles; inner bark made into twine or rope and used to weave trays, bags, and baskets.

TREE FACTS: Looks similar to the leaf on the Canadian flag; eriophyid mites, which attack the leaves of Douglas maple, provide an excellent food source for hummingbirds; also twigs are an important food source for ungulates.

(Acer circinatum Pursh) **vine maple**

APPEARANCE: A small tree up to 20 m; crooked trunk, often multi stemmed, lopsided crown.

OCCURRENCE: Coastal BC from Knight Inlet southward, rarely on Vancouver Island, found in a pocket in Wells Gray Park (240 km north of Kamloops), mid to lower elevations along streams.

BARK: Thin, smooth, pale green to dull brown with shallow crevices.

LEAVES: Opposite, deciduous, bright yellowish green, 7-9 lobes, single or double toothed, turns scarlet red in autumn before leaf fall.

FLOWERS: Clustered, purplish-red sepals and white petals, appear when leaves are half grown.

FRUITS: Wings 25-40 mm long, angle 180 degrees between them, seed case swollen and hairless, mature in late autumn.

WOOD: Heavy, fine grained; non commercial timber.

FIRST PEOPLES: Wood used for bows, floats for fishing nets, drum and cradle frames and snowshoes.

TREE FACTS: The name "vine" maple was probably derived from the gnarled and crooked appearance of the tree.

Oregon ash

(Fraxinus latifolia Benth.)*

APPEARANCE: A medium sized tree up to 27 m; tall trunk with spreading limbs.

OCCURRENCE: Recently discovered in BC, a few trees on Vancouver Island, Nahmint Valley, Pacific Rim National Park.

BARK: Young trees have rough bumps and grayish colour, deep crisscross cracks and reddish brown on older trees.

LEAVES: Opposite, compound, deciduous, light green.

FLOWERS: Small, male (yellowish) and female (greenish) flowers on separate trees, March-April blossoms.

FRUITS: Single wings (2.5-5.5 cm long), paddle shaped.

WOOD: Strong, tough wood; non commercial timber in BC.

FIRST PEOPLES: "Oregon ash sticks" were believed by some to offer protection from snakes as they would not slither over a stick from this tree.

TREE FACTS: *Fraxinus* Latin name for ash, from *phraxix* (a separation), referring to its use as European hedges.

Scientific Tree Names

In the scientific system of classification of all the world's living organisms, every species has its own two-parted name. (This is called "binomial nomenclature.") The name is derived from Latin, and begins with the *genus* name, followed by the *species* name. For example, all oaks have the genus name *Quercus*, and for each species of oak, a different *specific name* is used. Garry oak, the species that occurs in SW British Columbia, is named *Quercus garryana*. Red oak, an eastern North American species, is called *Quercus rubra*. Every other type of oak has a different species name. Similarly, all pines are named with the genus *Pinus*, with each different kind of pine having its own species name: *Pinus contorta* is lodgepole pine, *Pinus ponderosa* is ponderosa pine, and *Pinus monticola* is western white pine.

These scientific names are important for botanists and others trying to distinguish between different types of trees and other plants, because the common or local names that people use can vary from one region or country to another, and this can cause confusion. For example, "western redcedar" is the name used for *Thuja plicata* in western North America, but in some regions of North America, people use the name "redcedar" to refer to Rocky Mountain juniper *(Juniperus scopulorum)* and other juniper species. To avoid confusing these two different trees, botanists use their unique scientific names. After the Latin tree names is the last name of the first botanist who named the tree, followed by (in some cases) a second botanist who renamed the tree. Their names are usually abbreviated. The first time Douglas-fir is written in a scientific article it must appear in its entirety as "Douglas-fir *(Pseudotsuga menziesii* (Mirb.) Franco)." The Latin is italicized, and thereafter it can be written as either "Douglas-fir" or "*P. menziesii*" ("Douglas-fir" is hyphenated because it is not a "true fir" or *Abies*.) *Trees in Canada* (1995) by John Farrar has an excellent section explaining botanical authors and their abbreviations.

Brayshaw, T.C. 1996. *Trees and Shrubs of British Columbia*. Royal BC Museum, UBC Press, Vancouver.

Farrar, J. L. 1995. *Trees in Canada*. Canadian Forest Service, Fitzhenry & Whiteside, Markham, ON.

Lyons, C.P. and B. Marilees. 1995. *Trees, Shrubs & Flowers to Know in British Columbia & Washington*. Lone Pine Publishing, Vancouver and Edmonton.

MacKinnon, A., J. Pojar and R. Coupé. 1992. *Plants of Northern British Columbia.* Lone Pine Publishing, Vancouver and Edmonton.

Parish, R., R. Coupé and D. Lloyd. 1996. *Plants of Southern Interior British Columbia.* Lone Pine Publishing, Vancouver and Edmonton.

Pojar, J., & MacKinnon, A. (eds.). 1994. *Plants of Coastal British Columbia including Washington, Oregon & Alaska.* Lone Pine Publishing, Vancouver and Edmonton.

Turner, N. J. 1995. *Food Plants of Coastal First Peoples.* Royal British Columbia Museum Handbook, Victoria, B.C. (revised from 1975 edition, *Food Plants of British Columbia Indians.* Part 1. (*Coastal Peoples*), UBC Press, Vancouver.

Turner, N. J. 1997. *Food Plants of Interior First Peoples.* (Revised and Reissued Handbook orig. published in 1978 by B.C. Provincial Museum.) UBC Press, Vancouver and Royal British Columbia Museum, Victoria.

Turner, N. J. 1998. *Plant Technology of British Columbia First Peoples.* (Revised and Reissued Handbook, orig. published in 1979 by B.C. Provincial Museum.) UBC Press, Vancouver and Royal British Columbia Museum, Victoria.

Van Pelt, R. 2001. *Forest Giants of the Pacific Coast.* Global Forest Society, Banff, San Francisco and University of Washington Press, Seattle, London.

BOTANICAL NAME INDEX

Dr. Reese Halter is a research scientist (tree biology), conservationist, environmental speaker, TV documentary host, and children's author. He lives in Banff with his wife LuAn and their three children: Fred, Ryan and Jinji-Jo.
www.ReeseHalter.com

Dr. Nancy J. Turner is an ethnobotanist and professor in the School of Environmental Studies at the University of Victoria, Canada. She works with indigenous elders and plant specialists to document and promote their rich knowledge of the plant world.

GLOBAL FOREST

Pure Science.®

Global Forest Science (Dr. Reese Halter founder and president) is dedicated to conserving the world's forests through exploratory research and education. Its mission is to promote conservation of natural resources for future generations, providing vital information to corporate and governmental decision-makers and sharing the wonders of science and nature with children.

The proceeds of *Native Trees of BC* go towards basic scientific research on old growth forests and children's ecological education.

www.GlobalForestScience.org

GLOBAL FOREST

Pure Science. ®